A finely carved four-poster of c.1540 in the Henry VIII Room at Bretton Park, near Wakefield, West Yorkshire. The room, bed and panelling were re-sited in the new house built by Sir William Wentworth in 1720.

FOUR-POSTER AND TESTER BEDS

Ivan G. Sparkes

Shire Publications Ltd

CONTENTS

Printed in Great Britain by C. I. Thomas & Sons (Haverfordwest) Ltd, Press Buildings, Merlins Bridge, Haverfordwest, Dyfed SA61 1XF.

British Library Cataloguing in Publication Data: Sparkes, Ivan G. (Ivan George). Four-poster and tester beds. 1. English beds, history. I. Title. 749.3. ISBN 0-7478-0078-2.

ACKNOWLEDGEMENTS
The author and publishers acknowledge with gratitude the assistance of the following in the preparation of the book: the staff of the reference department of High Wycombe Central Library; The Adshop, Halesworth, for photocopying; David Youens of Keens (Commercial), High Wycombe; Cyril Roberts of High Wycombe; the Victoria and Albert Museum; Mary Brooks of York Castle Museum; and the staff of the hotels listed on pages 31 and 32, who helped with information and illustrations.

Cover: *Eighteenth-century bed embroidered with the coat of arms and royal cipher of George III in the Ambassador's Room at Scone Palace, near Perth, Scotland.*

The parts of a four-poster or tester bed.

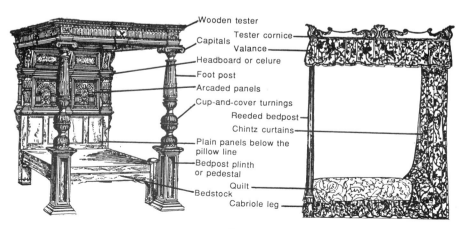

Wooden tester
Tester cornice
Capitals
Valance
Headboard or celure
Foot post
Arcaded panels
Cup-and-cover turnings
Reeded bedpost
Chintz curtains
Plain panels below the pillow line
Bedpost plinth or pedestal
Quilt
Bedstock
Cabriole leg

The hung bed with a fabric tester hung from the rafters. The curtains at the foot of the bed are looped up in the form of a bag, c.1480. (British Museum, Harley MS 4431.)

THE MEDIEVAL HUNG BED 1200-1500

In the early medieval period the lord of the manor and his household ate and slept in the great hall of the manor house, but as the middle ages progressed the lord and his family sought more privacy. The first move was to create an alcove with hangings suspended from the ceiling or walls, in a similar manner to those used in hospital cubicles today, thus forming the *hung bed*. During the thirteenth century the bedstead was set under a more sophisticated fabric canopy called a *tester* suspended from the rafters, and the bed curtains hung from this canopy. A link between this tester and the bedstead itself was created by dropping a piece of fabric down in front of the wall behind the sleeper's head,

which matched the cloth used in the rest of the bed. This was called a *celure* and it eventually formed the bedhead of later centuries. The bedstead, often called a *bedstock*, consisted of four low rails drilled with holes through which cords could be threaded to form a loose network on which a mattress of plaited rushes could be laid.

A distinction was drawn between the bed, which consisted of the bedclothes, mattresses, tester and curtains, and the bedstock, which was the wooden framework which supported them. It was common practice for the curtains to hang from the tester on rings which ran on iron rods, and in daytime, when the bed was used as a couch or seat, the curtains

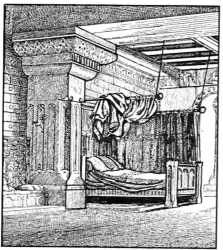

The medieval bed with curtains at the side (thirteenth century). (From E. E. Viollet-le-Duc, 'Dictionary of French Furniture', 1868.)

In the middle ages development was concentrated not on the wooden structure of the bed but on the draperies to keep out the cold. These might be so costly and precious that they were passed from father to son. Ralph, Lord Barrett, in his will of 1389, stipulated that he who 'shall first bear my surname and arms, according to my will, shall have the use of my great velvet bed for life'.

A canopy used over chairs, thrones or beds was a mark of privilege, known as a *canopy of state;* when it extended over the whole bed it indicated high honour to a guest, while the half-tester was used as a lesser mark of deference. State beds of the fifteenth century were not necessarily used for sleeping but formed part of the trappings of court ceremony, used for private audiences with favoured visitors. Although the rectangular tester was the normal form of canopy, another shape favoured at this time was conical, like a bell tent, and called a *sparver.*

The materials used in the manufacture of draperies for these beds were very rich. Italy was producing silk velvet as early as 1247 and sumptuous fabrics were soon exported to other parts of Europe for use in churches and great houses. Bedchambers were sometimes hung with tapestries and early inventories occasionally mention beds with hangings of wor-

would be gathered together and folded up in the form of a bag. The hung bed was in use from the thirteenth century to the fifteenth and became a symbol of prestige and wealth. In 1412 the will of Roger Kyrkby, vicar of Gaiford, mentioned 'one bed in conformity with his position'.

Illustration of the hung bed with the curtains down on one side and at the foot. The low wooden bedhead can be seen above the pillow, c.1485. (Book of Hours, British Museum Add MS 17012 F2.)

The medieval chamber in which the bed takes its place with other furniture. It has a sparver or tent-shaped tester and is being used as an audience chamber, c.1485. (British Museum, Harley MS 4373. F886)

sted fabric woven on English looms at King's Lynn and Norwich. Some less rich draperies were probably made of woollen cloth or linen, either plain or embroidered with small flowers, plant forms or heraldic devices.

Although hangings suspended from the ceiling remained in favour up to 1600, increasingly they were superseded by testers or canopies carried on the frame of the bed itself. This change came slowly and was not fully accepted before the end of the fifteenth century.

In the early stages of this transition, the hung bed consisted of the curtain fabric draped over a suspended wooden tester frame, with the celure or fabric bedhead dropped below it. Next came the *posted bedstead* with the tester, which might be either a wooden frame or fabric hangings, supported by four posts instead of suspended from the rafters, and the fabric celure hanging down between the two head posts. Then the fabric celure was replaced by a wooden panelled and carved bedhead which was joined to the two head posts, which, with the two foot posts, supported the tester. This type is loosely termed a four-poster bed, although only two posts stand free. Finally the head posts disappear and the wooden celure and the two foot posts support a panelled wooden tester, creating a substantial structure known as a *wainscot* or *standing bed*.

An oak four-poster of c.1600, with high foot plinth and cup-and-cover carving on the upper part of the foot posts, which stand separate from the bedstock. (Billesley Manor Hotel, near Alcester, Warwickshire)

THE FOUR-POST BED 1500-1650

Between 1500 and 1550 the wooden framework of the bed was taking on new importance. The wooden panelled headboard had come into use, replacing the fabric celure at the bedhead. The oak of which it was made was often imported from Scandinavia and as this timber was also used in the panelling of walls and ceilings the headboard was generally known as the wainscot, although because similar panels were used in sealing the roof or wall this type of bed was called a *sealed bed* in the Elizabethan period. At first these beds were confined to the wealthy, but soon they were introduced to the homes of yeomen farmers. They remained popular until the middle of the seventeenth century and were variously known at the time as sealed beds, posted bedsteads or wainscot beds. The term *four-poster* was not used until the nineteenth century.

At first the bedposts were square or hexagonal in section, carved with geometrical patterns such as chevrons. They had bosses two-thirds of the way up, on which could be carved family initials or emblems. Soon this elegance was displaced by exuberant Elizabethan carving.

Throughout the sixteenth century designs for beds became more architectural, particularly after furniture pattern books began to appear in the second half of the century. After 1560 substantial foot posts with heavy wooden bulbs on massive free-standing pedestals and plinths of square section were in favour. By 1575 the posts were designed with the cup-and-cover motif and were carved with gadrooning, strapwork and acanthus leaves. Some late seventeenth-century examples used architectural designs, with fluted shafts topped by Ionic capitals. The foot posts became an integral part of the bedstead by 1600; hitherto they had often been separate from the bed, standing a few inches in front of the low framework.

The tester was made of wood, panelled on the underside and decorated with a frieze, or *cornice*, of heavy carving. The celure would be plain below the pillow line, but above it there was arcaded decoration in the form of pilasters and carved figures. The panels so created were inlaid with marquetry in bog-oak, holly, box, poplar and sycamore, and they were described by Paul Hentzner in 1578 as 'ingeniously composed of wood of different colours'. The carving used on these beds changed in style by the 1650s, becoming more formal and restrained. By the end of the seventeenth century, the very heavy sealed beds were going out of fashion.

The most famous example is the Great Bed of Ware, which can be seen in the Victoria and Albert Museum, London. This was probably made for Sir Henry Fanshaw of Ware Park in about 1600, but by 1612 it had been transferred to the White Hart Inn, Ware, Hertfordshire. It was moved from inn to inn in the town until 1869, when it was removed to Rye House, Hoddesdon, Hertfordshire. It is 10 feet 8 inches (3.25 metres) square and stands 8 feet 9 inches (2.67 metres) high, and, according to Sir Henry Chauncey's *History of Hertford* (1700), bedded 'six citizens and their wives . . . from London'. Such a size was not unusual: the royal beds of Henry VII, Henry VIII and Edward VI were quoted as being 11 feet (3.35 metres) square when on display at Windsor in 1598.

The bedstock itself was low, the side rails being holed and grooved for the

Left: *An early oak four-poster bed, c.1530, with octagonal foot posts which stand in front of the bedstock, which itself forms part of the bedhead or celure, which has lost the head posts. Note the two carved bosses two-thirds of the way up the bedposts. (From Crackenthorpe Hall, near Appleby, Cumbria, now in the Victoria and Albert Museum.)*

Right: *An oak four-poster of c.1540-50, which still has the head posts flanking the panelled bedhead. The foot posts have chevron carving. Note the holes bored in the bed rails for the mattress cords.*

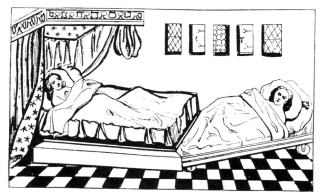

cord lacing which secured the canvas bed hammock but also tightened the mortices in the corner posts. The mattresses were made of carded wool in the sixteenth century, with the best ones filled with swan's down. Flock was cheaper, while John Evelyn in 1664 recommends 'the leaves of beech being gathered about the fall and somewhat before they are frost bitten'. The total bedding consisted of a pallet of straw or wool covered with canvas, two feather-beds, sheets, blankets, another feather-bed acting as an eiderdown, and over all an embroidered quilt. These feather-beds were common in well furnished houses but considered a luxury until the sixteenth century for the poorer classes, whose beds had usually consisted of a straw pallet covered only with a sheet. An inventory of 1660 mentions 'little trundel beds under the greate beds, which were for the gentleman's men'. These were simple low bedstocks on wooden wheels, which

An oak four-poster of c.1600 with plain panelled bedhead and heavily turned foot posts with cup-and-cover bulbous carving. (Seckford Hall Hotel, Woodbridge, Suffolk.)

The Great Bed of Ware, c.1600, 10 feet 8 inches (3.25 metres) square and 8 feet 9 inches (2.67 metres) high, showing its remarkable carved figures and arcaded marquetry architectural picture. (Victoria and Albert Museum.)

could be pushed out of sight under the main bedstead during the day. Although still in use into the nineteenth century, they went out of fashion in the eighteenth century as rooms for domestic staff were created in the attics.

The luxury fabrics used in the curtains and coverings of the beds of the rich in the sixteenth century were still purchased abroad, but after the Dissolution of the Monasteries the skill of the English embroiderers began to be directed to secular work. Crewel embroidery was in daily use, worked in coloured wools on a closely woven ground. As the sixteenth century advanced, the production of Italian woven silk fabrics increased, and these were lighter and more ornamental

in design. The importation of painted or printed cotton cloth from India was allowed in 1631. This fabric, which later developed a glazed stiff finish, was called *chint* in Hindi, meaning 'spotted cloth'. It came to be typified by a white ground with branches and flowers, a design and fabric which were speedily prepared for the European market, and became known as chintz. It was also in time produced in England, for in 1676 William Sherwin received a Crown grant for a 'new and speedy way for printing broad cloth'. Samuel Pepys records in his *Diary* that he bought some 'chint' in 1663 for his wife to line her new study. It was not widely used for bed hangings until the eighteenth century.

Above left: *State bed made for the town house of Sir Dudley North, c.1685, covered with crimson velvet, tassel-fringed, with vase and feathers surmounting the tester at each corner.*

Above right: *William III's state bed at Hampton Court.*

Below left: *A canopy of state from Hampton Court, c.1700.*

Below right: *Queen Anne's state bed in Spitalfields silk-velvet, c.1714, at Hampton Court.*

Stuart beds: (top left and right) the James II Suite, at Knole, Kent; (bottom right) state bed in the style of Marot, 1695; (bottom left) Queen Mary's bed, c.1690, at Hampton Court.

THE STATE BED 1660-1720

While the wooden four-poster was in fashion from 1500 to 1675, the hung bed of the previous era was still a prestige item and used on great occasions. The draperies were no longer hung from the ceiling by ropes, and the bed became called a *covered bed,* because the woodwork supporting the bed itself was hidden, as the draperies once more predominated. This new bed had evolved a lighter framework, a deep tester valance, tall slender posts and a headboard covered with rich and colourful fabrics. In the early seventeenth century highly decorated upholstered beds of European design in baroque style came into England with tester cornices surmounted by ornately carved and pierced cresting. With the return of Charles II from France at the Restoration in 1660 ideas flooded into England and the covered bed became established.

Lit de Marie Antoinette

Lit à l'impériale   Lit à la turque   Lit à la romaine

Lit en tombeau   Lit à la dauphine   Lit d'ange   Lit à la duchesse

Varieties of French bed designs which influenced English craftsmen, c.1680-1730.

By the time of William III, the posts and panels of the celure and tester were covered with silk damask or figured velvet. Trimmings of silver added to the richness of their appearance. As architectural designs changed, the lofty rooms of the Stuart period made the old-fashioned Elizabethan beds appear dwarfed, and the new design for state beds which towered to 16 or 18 feet (4.8-5.5 metres) looked more suitable. In the wealthier houses walnut was used for the great beds, embellished with intricate carving. Other beds were made of beech or deal and painted, or of pine and covered with gesso and gilded. The height of these massive beds was exaggerated even more by the use of tall pinnacles or gilt cups holding ostrich plumes, set at each corner above the cresting. Such plumes could be expensive. In an earlier period John Evelyn wrote of a French duchess who spent 'near a thousand pounds of our money upon tufts of plumes to decorate a bed'. The grooming of these plumes required a 'feather dresser' to be

employed at Windsor Castle to look after them.

The draperies of the bed, which included the valance, tester, curtains and quilt, were usually of matching material, and it was now proper for the chamber to be hung with wall cloths, panels of which were called *costers*. The French fashion of having chairs and stools in the bedchamber matching the bed fabric became established in England in about 1670, although as early as 1620 the Spangled Bed at Knole, Kent, had an *en suite* set of stools and an X-frame chair. This French influence became more pronounced when the celebrated designer Daniel Marot became architect to William III. A number of his designs were accepted by the King, and they strongly influenced other bed upholsterers. Between 1699 and 1701 Hampton Court was largely refurbished for William III. This included renewing the fabrics of the canopies of state under which the King's throne was placed when he received dignitaries in audience. For these a rich crimson

12

Genoa damask was used, trimmed with gold lace and silk fringes. Similar materials were used for William's state bed, and an upholsterer's bill of the period shows that a state bed required 321 yards (294 metres) of velvet at 42 shillings a yard, 81 yards (74 metres) of satin at 10 shillings a yard, 336 yards (307 metres) of broad lace at 3s 4d a yard and 402 yards (368 metres) of narrow lace at 2s 9d a yard, making a total in excess of £826, with the make-up charge (1714) at £25. To manage beds of such height required special equipment, so a joiner was required to provide a long pole with a hook and ferrule to 'turn the curtains'.

For most people fustian (a fabric of mixed fibres, usually cotton and linen) and stained cloth (usually linen, painted in imitation of tapestry) were common, and other materials for even humbler beds included worsted, counterfeit baudekin, which was an imitation silk brocade, and linen. Printed and painted hangings were arriving from India and later from China. European interpretations of Chinese designs became very popular and typical motifs were incorporated in many forms of decoration. The style became known as *chinoiserie*. England became an important producer of silk cloth when many Huguenots came over from France following the revocation of the Edict of Nantes in 1685. The

Left: *Half-tester or angel bed, c.1710, with serpentine cornice, the tester hung by chains from the ceiling. (Leeds Castle, Kent.)*

Below: *A bed with fabric tester, c.1720, low bedhead and posts crudely shaped on square foot plinths. The use of chintz lightens the appearance of the bed. (Bailiffscourt Hotel, Climping, Littlehampton, West Sussex.)*

largest colony of French workers settled in Spitalfields, London, where they carried on their weaving well into the nineteenth century.

The feather-bed of the rich was still swan's down, while lower mattresses were filled with wool or straw. These were piled high on the bed for comfort, and a set of portable steps was necessary in order to get into the bed.

In 1730 J. Southall commented '. . . bugs have been known in England above sixty years, and every season increasingly so upon us as to become terrible to almost every inhabitant . . .' It was not until the introduction of cheap cotton bed linen in the nineteenth century that the bugs could be boiled to death without spoiling the sheets. Such afflictions could be taken calmly, as Samuel Pepys shows, for he 'came about ten at night to a little inn . . . and the wife and I lay up, finding our bed good but lousy, which made us merry'.

The bed had long been part of the furniture of the downstairs living or reception room, and it was not until the seventeenth century that it was to be found on the first floor. As late as the eighteenth century the ground-floor bedroom was still not unusual, and in Edinburgh new town houses were designed with a downstairs bedroom in the late eighteenth century.

EARLY GEORGIAN BEDS 1720-50

The early Georgian style had certain architectural features which were linked to the Palladian designs of such architects as William Kent. He used classical mouldings, repetitive ornament, fluted pilasters and Corinthian capitals. Mahogany, introduced in the 1720s, began to oust walnut and oak, particularly after Sir Robert Walpole repealed the import duty on it in 1733. It was a more versatile wood which allowed a greater elaboration of carved details than had been possible in walnut. The Georgian bed with its shaped and carved mahogany tester was to become the model for many years and was accepted as the *tester bed*, a term used well into the mid Victorian period. In beds we find the cornice free of its fabric covering, and in the 1730s the foot posts were revealed once again, showing a design of lighter, simpler classical lines. The height of the bed was reduced, but the draperies on the headboard were retained in some instances until the 1780s, with the fabric often glued in folds on the wood.

The bases of the new slender foot posts were uncovered, and in the 1720s the cabriole leg, which had been introduced into chair design about 1700, began to support the bed posts. From 1740 the panelled headboard was reintroduced, and the cornice of the tester was often carved, frequently with acanthus leaves. The foot posts were turned and carved in low relief above the mattress, having vase-shaped plinths below, and after about 1750 the earlier cabriole leg was omitted and a small square plinth added to a square post. The head posts were plain, square and tapered, as they were intended to be hidden by curtains. The side and end rails of the bedstead were tenoned into the four corner posts and secured with coach screws. A series of wooden laths replaced the earlier roped-on canvas mattress.

The half-tester, in which the canopy covered only about half of the bed area, reappeared in about 1700 and was sometimes known as an *angel bed*. The front of the half-tester was not supported by posts, but the shorter framework was fixed to timbers forming the back of the bed or often secured to the ceiling with chains. In most cases it was possible to enclose the sleeper by pulling the curtain around the half-tester, but some versions had side curtains only. Celia Fiennes, writing in 1702, saw at Windsor two bed-chambers, 'one with a half bedstead as the new mode'.

Another lighter structure was the *field bed,* which was made to fold up for travelling. It was also listed in medieval inventories, and one made for the Earl of

Above: *Georgian covered bed, c.1735, with low upholstered bedhead, deep valance and fringed and tasselled full curtains. (Royal Crescent Hotel, Bath.)*

Below left: *Mahogany tester bed in architectural style with fluted posts and Corinthian capitals, c.1740. (Victoria and Albert Museum.)*

Below right: *Magnificent state bed designed by the architect William Kent in 1732, hung with green velvet embroidered with gold. Height 16 feet (4.9 metres). (Houghton Hall, Norfolk.)*

Mahogany field bed with chintz hangings, mid eighteenth century. A lighter bed for the smaller room, made of sections which could be dismantled.

Leicester in 1588 was carved and gilded and fitted with draperies of green and purple satin and gold. The government also used them, as a Treasury warrant of 1729 ordered 'four four-post field bedsteads of crimson harateen [worsted] furniture, with complete sets of bedding'. They consisted of a sloped rising roof or tent made of curved rods supported on the top of four posts, the whole masked by draperies and gathered curtains. These could be packed up, as was necessary for a travelling bed. The *yeoman's bed* was rather simpler, still clinging to the four-post tradition of the previous century. The posts would be square below the mattress and were turned above, ending in metal spikes which supported the tester. Bed rails were drilled for cords to retain the mattresses, and the bedposts would be linked by iron curtain rails which could be held in position by metal eyes. Although most cottage furniture would be made locally, the inventory of a resident of Durham included 'two London bedsteads and one new London table'.

London was the place to buy materials for re-covering beds, and in 1735 Elizabeth Purefoy sent for patterns of quilting 'at the lowest prices of each pattern'. She bought 45 yards at 10s 6d a yard, while her husband bought 4 yards of thick plain white dimity to make some nightcaps. Crewel embroidery remained much in fashion for the draperies, using designs of sprays of flowers, such as carnations or honeysuckle, patterns also used on furniture covers and quilts. In 1701 Parliament prohibited the importation of printed chintzes from India and domestic fabric printing greatly increased. A second act, in 1720, prohibited the import of all printed, painted, stained and dyed cotton calicoes (except blue). English manufacturers began to block-print on fustians (linen and cotton) using established Indienne and chinoiserie designs. During this period the silk-weaving looms in England were fully employed, and the heavier materials such as velvet were no longer considered suitable for the lighter furniture and the more delicate treatment of the woodwork.

Georgian mahogany tester bed, c.1750, with panelled bedhead and tester, vase turnings at the base of the foot posts and pedestals terminating in cabriole legs.

16

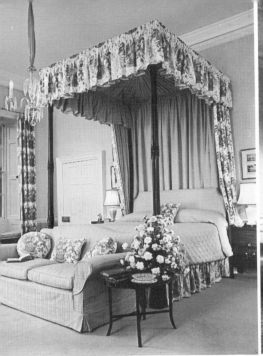

Left: *A Chippendale four-poster with cluster columns. Originally made for Corsham Court, Wiltshire, the bed has since been re-dressed with new fabrics created for the National Trust. (Ston Easton Park, Bath.)*

Right: *Chippendale mahogany bed with serpentine cornice and deep valance, c.1755. (Tabley House, Knutsford, Cheshire.)*

THE LATE GEORGIAN DESIGNER BED 1750-1805

By 1740 most good-quality furniture was being made of mahogany and a style of furniture began to evolve which was English in character though influenced by the rococo styles of carved florid festoons, rockwork and garlands which originated in the France of Louis XV. The tester bed with tall slender posts had superseded the covered bed, with a richly carved mahogany headboard and foot posts often in cluster form, like church columns.

Designers began to have a greater influence as attitudes to furnishing the bedroom altered. Among their designs of furniture to suit the fashionable tastes of those who could afford them, they offered a wide range of beds, often in conjunction with other furnishings and sometimes taking into account an indi-vidual room. Towards the end of this period other types of bed, which had mainly developed from the elaborate chaise-longue or day-bed, began to appear, such as canopied couches, sofa beds and the French *bateau* (boat) bed.

Thomas Chippendale (1718-79) was the first of a new generation of designers. A cabinet-maker working in London, he published in 1754 the *Gentleman and Cabinet-maker's Director* containing designs for both ordinary and elaborate furniture. This was possibly the first time that such a book had been offered showing pieces that could be made even by the country craftsman and it had great influence. As well as rococo elements, Chippendale used popular Chinese features. The fine chinoiserie bed at the Victoria and Albert Museum, originally thought

17

Chippendale bed designs (from left to right): (top) canopy bed; state bed; serpentine bed; (bottom) Gothick bed; Chinese bed at the Victoria and Albert Museum (now attributed to William Linnell); dome bed.

to be by Chippendale, is now attributed to William Linnell. This is decorated with a pagoda-shaped canopy and a gilt dragon on each corner post. The *Director* includes a 'Chinese sopha' with pagoda canopy and decoration and other items that were 'Chinese or in Chinese taste'. Chippendale's two 'Gothic beds' incorporate tracery work, Gothic cusping and cluster columns and reflect the increasing interest in medieval styles.

Some of the finest work from Chippendale's own workshop was made to the refined classical designs of Robert Adam (1728-92), the architect and designer who led the classical movement based

on Roman and Italian models which displaced rococo. Classical outlines appeared light and delicate, with tapering columns and balanced curves, and Adam created a simple elegant style which influenced or was copied by other designers beyond the end of the eighteenth century and ultimately affected every field of the creative arts.

Adam's designs gained an even wider public through George Hepplewhite (died 1786), who is known mainly because of his illustrations in his book *The Cabinet-maker's and Upholsterer's Guide*, first published by his widow in 1788. At about the same time (1791-4)

Thomas Sheraton published his *Cabinet-maker's and Upholsterer's Drawing Book*, which provides a comprehensive picture of good-quality furniture at the end of the eighteenth century.

The mahogany bed in use at the end of the eighteenth century reflects the designs of both Hepplewhite and Sheraton. The foot posts had a vase-shaped swelling which was similar to the vase motif which appears in Robert Adam's designs, and this led to the reeded or fluted tapered post. The cornice, surmounting a painted and tabbed valance, was carved mahogany or had painted decoration. The draperies were described by Hepplewhite as plain or figured silk and satins with fringed velvet for state beds, printed cottons, plain or corded white dimity with a fringe of gimpthread known as 'Manchester stuff' for other beds. If the valance was gathered fully, it was known as a *petticoat valance*. Printed cottons were produced after 1770 from incised copper plates which gave a fineness of detail. In 1796 the engraved roller was first introduced, and by this process a machine could print some 4000 yards (3700 metres) of material a day. Mechanical engraving was available in 1801, and all these inventions enabled cheaper cottons to be produced, bringing them within the

Design by Robert Adam for a dome bed for Osterley Park, 1775.

reach of many more people in the nineteenth century.

Thomas Sheraton's work is distinguished by its slender form and elegance. He abandoned to a large extent

Hepplewhite bed designs: (from left to right) canopied bed in classic style; dome bedstead with scalloped valance; draped canopy bedstead; draped mahogany tester bed.

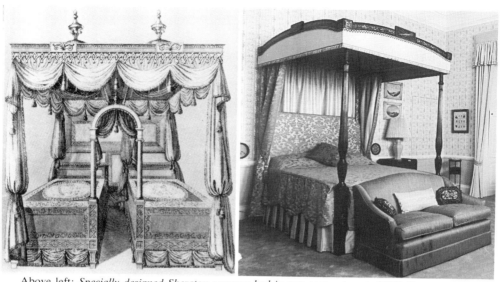

Above left: *Specially designed Sheraton summer bed in two compartments (1791-4).*

Above right: *Period Hepplewhite bed, with painted cornice, plain valance with fringe, and upholstered bedhead. (Ston Easton Park, Bath.)*

Below left: *Matching single half-tester beds in Indian print counterpanes, covers and curtains. (Château du Buzay.)*

Below right: *Gilt four-poster, c.1765, the posts and cornice designed as palm trees, with the curving branches spreading above and below the plain valance. (Kedleston Hall, Derbyshire.)*

Sheraton bed designs: (top left) a sofa bed, framed in white and gold, also called a French bed; (top right) a draped bed; (bottom left) a French state bed; (bottom right) an English state bed.

the curved lines and contours reintroduced by Hepplewhite and, like Robert Adam, favoured the straight line. Sheraton looked back to Chippendale and commented that his designs 'are now wholly antiquated and laid aside', adding that 'time alters fashions'. His drawings for the furniture of the 1790s were plainer and lighter than earlier designs. Mahogany had largely given way to satinwood, which had been brought to England from India in about 1760. It was used in veneer form from about 1780, and it had a cool, light and pleasing effect. The bedsteads in Sheraton's *Drawing Book* appear more unusual than typical of the period and include the 'alcove bed', the 'summer bed in two compartments' and the 'elliptic bed'. He seemed to admire the design which used a domed tester or cupola linked to elaborate draperies and valances, which were festooned, braided and betasselled.

Bed designs by George Smith: (top left) military officer's bed; (top right) Gothick state bed; (bottom left) polonaise bed; (bottom right) Regency dome bed.

REGENCY AND VICTORIAN BEDS 1805-90

The Regency period brought a change from the clean lines of the late Georgian style to the heavier, often over-decorated furniture of designers who led the way to the florid Victorian style. Draperies were necessary to give privacy, so in the early Regency the satins, silk damask and chintz materials were still in use. Later, lighter materials were popular. John C. Loudon in 1833 commented that chintz was preferred for bed curtains as 'it admits of being washed' and dimity, a light cotton fabric, was used because curtains made of this 'keep long clean'. Tent beds were still in use and they changed their form little during the first half of the nineteenth century.

The four-poster bed, and to some extent the tent bed, were increasingly replaced by the French *bateau* bed, which was similar to a Grecian sofa. A pole projected from the wall behind the couch at a height of 10 feet (3 metres), and the draperies were hung over it. The couch or sofa was often boat-shaped with scrolled-over ends, made of mahogany and enriched with brass ornament in classical taste. One of the first design books to have an impact at this time was *Collection of Designs for Household Furniture and Interior Decoration* by George Smith, published in 1808. It included an array of four-posters, half-testers and French beds, often with extravagant draperies. The military bed had its curtain hanging from crossed swords. The state bed, which now found its place in the main bedroom of most country houses, appears here within a stone Gothic arch using pinnacles for bedposts, while the *polonaise* bed with its central dome and carefully arranged hangings bears a strong resemblance to Sheraton's French bed of a decade earlier. The footboard, which was framed between the foot posts of the bed, came into use about 1810 and remained an integral part of the bed, in its many forms, until after the Second World War, when the divan bed made its appearance.

Smith's ideas of the Gothic were pushed further by Augustus Pugin, whose *Gothic Furniture in the Style of the Fifteenth Century* (1835) re-created the elaborate woodwork of Perpendicular architecture in what he termed his 'florid style'. Much simpler were the beds recommended in Loudon's *Encyclopedia of Cottage, Farm and Villa Architecture and Furniture* (first edition 1833), which dealt with designs more suitable for the middle classes. Loudon felt that the idea of metal bedsteads 'would shock those who have always been accustomed to consider mahogany essential'. But it seems that before the Great Exhibition of 1851 only some four hundred brass beds were made a week, while after they had been exhibited there more than five thousand a week were manufactured.

By 1851 the use of the fully curtained bed had declined to such an extent that a writer in 1877 commented: 'now that the venerable four-post bedstead is generally discarded, the mahogany half-tester has taken its place'. The pages of Loudon's *Encyclopedia* include quite a number of half-testers, both of wood and of metal, but it is in the design books or catalogues of designers and manufacturers such as Thomas King (1839) and William Smee and Sons (1850) and in Blackie's *Cabinetmaker's Assistant* (1859) that we see their increasing popularity. Later, with Richard Charles (1866-8), the elaborate half-tester in eighteenth-century style reappears, while the designs of G. W. Yapp (1876) show an elaboration which almost exceeds the extravagances of the Stuart state beds. The half-tester continued through designs by G. Maddox (1882), an Adam reconstruction by James Shoolbred and Company (1889) and the Army and Navy catalogue (1880) almost into the twentieth century. Occasionally a designer attempted to direct fashion, such as Charles Eastlake in 1878 with his iron half-tester bedsteads painted in Venetian red, chocolate or sage green, with striped

Left: *Regency canopy bed, c.1820. (Riber Hall, Matlock, Derbyshire.)*

Right: *Nineteenth-century pitch-pine four-poster, completely covered in green Fortuni fabric. The bed was a state bed from a Welsh castle. (Ston Easton Park, Bath.)*

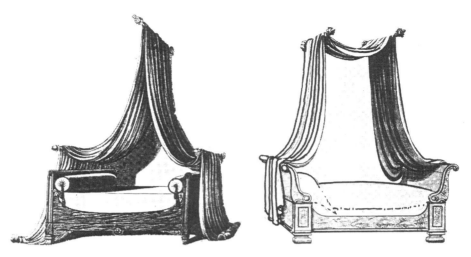

Left: *French bed with draperies supported by one wall-pole over a Turkish-style divan, designed by George Smith, 1826.*

Right: *French bed with draperies hung between two wall-poles over a Grecian-style bed, designed by Thomas King, 1839.*

Below: *Types of bed posts: (left) sixteenth-century; (centre) eighteenth-century; (right) nineteenth-century.*

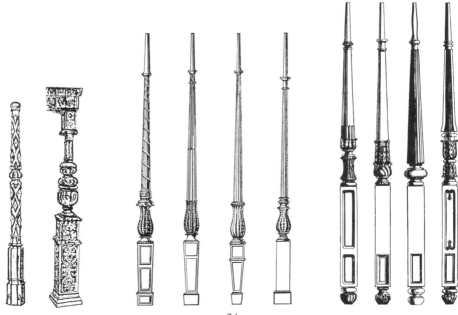

Nineteenth-century bed designs: (top, from left to right) draped bedstead by Thomas King, 1839; half-tester by Charles Eastlake, 1878; state bed by John Braund, 1858; (bottom left) papier-mâché half-tester, 1850; (bottom right) design of Victorian brass bedstead fitted with a 'corona' for the tent-shaped draperies, c.1840.

masculine hangings suspended on projecting spears. A patent of 1842 enabled metal and wood to be covered with japanned papier-mâché, thus allowing beds such as half-testers to be made of this material.

By 1875 the metal bedstead was in general use, and some six thousand brass bedsteads a week were made in Birmingham. The use of metal was advised on health grounds, and, as many were still produced to carry draperies, the bed posts and tester frames could be thinner and lighter in appearance. The mattress was supported on stout metal laths which replaced the wooden laths and corded lacing by 1850. The spring mattress became available in 1855, and the tension wire mattress by 1890.

A large number of straightforward wooden four-poster beds were still made, and the design books carried them up to the 1880s. Many of the designs harked back to the great designers. John

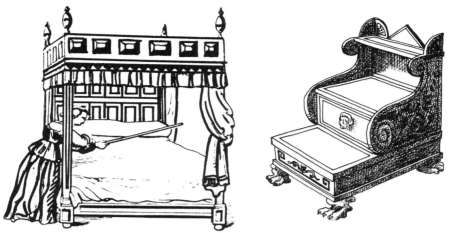

Left: *The bed staff in use for smoothing the bed covers, 1631. It appears that earlier it was used in France to poke and thwack the bedding, to ensure that no intruder was hiding there.*

Right: *A set of elaborate bed steps with central drawer, c.1860.*

Below: *From the late sixteenth century the chambermaid would warm the bed with a warming pan filled with charcoal or hot embers from the fire. The seventeenth-century example (above) is of brass throughout but from about 1730 they were made mainly of copper with wooden turned handles (below).*

Bottom: *An eighteenth-century alternative to the warming pan was the bed wagon, a light wooden framework within which a pan of hot charcoal was suspended.*

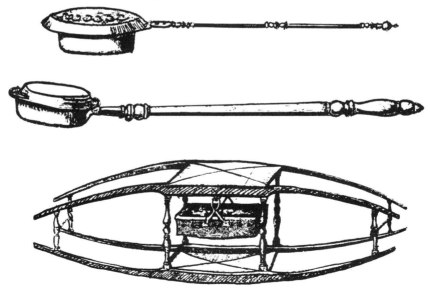

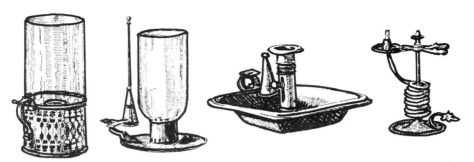

Bedlights: (from left to right) two late eighteenth-century brass bedroom candlesticks with glass funnels; early nineteenth-century brass open candlestick with cone-shaped snuffer; late eighteenth-century brass taper holder.

Braund in 1858 produced a design of a state bed not unlike the Marot style of the seventeenth century. John Taylor in 1850 used drapery, tasselled cornices and valances to give the rich effect of the 1780s, while G. W. Yapp in 1879 was producing designs of heavily carved tent beds and Gothic tester beds similar to those which appeared in the design books of the Gothic revivals of the 1770s and 1830s.

The four-poster and half-tester bed which had evolved and changed over the years appeared to have fulfilled its purpose by the late nineteenth century. Many, however, have survived and can

Above: *The chambermaid warming a bed with the warming-pan. Note the crude bed steps next to the bed.*

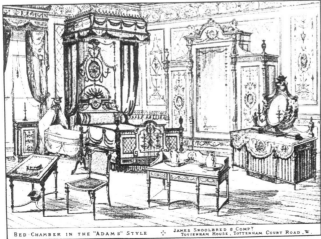

BED·CHAMBER IN THE "ADAMS" STYLE ⁖ JAMES SHOOLBRED & COMPᵧ TOTTENHAM HOUSE, TOTTENHAM COURT ROAD, W.

Left: *Bedchamber in Adam style, with half-tester bed, illustrated in the 1889 catalogue of James Shoolbred and Company.*

Beds illustrated in the Army and Navy Co-operative Society Catalogue, 1880: (upper left) tent bed; (upper right) French bed; (lower left) half-tester bed; (lower right) four-poster bed.

be seen in museums, stately homes and hotels. Nowadays there is a revival in interest: both wooden and brass examples appear in the catalogues of manufacturers, and even do-it-yourself stores offer a four-poster frame in pine for the home designer. But for most people, the best chance of sleeping in a four-poster is to stay at one of the hotels which provide this type of bed as a luxury attraction.

Left: *Victorian mahogany bed, c.1850, with panelled bedhead and tester, valance and side curtains. (Chesterfield Hotel, Bath.)*

Right: *Reproduction Elizabethan four-poster with plain panelled bedhead and footboard, and matching floral valance, quilt and base frill. (Oakleaf Reproduction, Bradford.)*

Below: *Fabrics used for bed hangings. (From left to right) Elizabethan embroidery, using scrolls, sweet peas, honeysuckle, roses and other flowers, worked in coloured silks or silver-gilt and silver thread; crewel embroidery, c.1650: sometimes this was worked in one colour such as dark green in a thin worsted yarn, but colours such as blue, yellow, green and red were embroidered in a material composed of linen warp and cotton weft; example of Florentine velvet of the fifteenth century: the velvet is a rich red on a ground of gold, imported into England during the early years of the sixteenth century; damask woven at Spitalfields in the eighteenth century.*

Types of four-poster and tester bed (from left to right): (top row) the hung bed; Elizabethan four-poster; Stuart covered or state bed; (upper centre) Georgian canopy bed; mahogany tester bed; Georgian Gothick bed; Georgian canopy bed; (lower centre) French bed; camp bed; dome bed; (bottom row) tent or field bed; Victorian brass half-tester bed; Victorian half-tester bed.

FURTHER READING

Fastnedge, Ralph. *English Furniture Styles from 1500 to 1830.* Herbert Jenkins, 1962.
Joy, Edward, *et al. Pictorial Dictionary of British Nineteenth Century Furniture Design.* Antique Collector's Club, 1977. Contains a list of design books and catalogues.
Macquoid, Percy, and Edwards, Ralph. *The Dictionary of English Furniture.* Country Life, 1924-7; revised edition 1954.
Sparkes, Ivan G. *Illustrated History of English Domestic Furniture 1100-1837.* Spurbooks, 1980.
Strange, Thomas Arthur. *A Guide to Collections.* McCorquodale, undated. 3500 illustrations of English furniture from the last half of the seventeenth century to the early part of the nineteenth.
Wolsey, S. W., and Luff, R. W. P. *Furniture in England: the Age of the Joiner.* Arthur Barker, 1968.
Wright, Lawrence. *Warm and Snug: the History of the Bed.* Routledge and Kegan Paul, 1962.

PLACES TO VISIT

Four-poster and tester beds may be seen in historic houses open to the public, inns and hotels. Museums may have examples, but because of the size of these beds only larger museums, such as the Victoria and Albert Museum in South Kensington, London, or specialist museums, such as Temple Newsam, Leeds, have a range which illustrates the variety produced over the centuries. Palaces such as Hampton Court, Middlesex, and most of the larger stately homes are furnished with them.

Nowadays it is often possible to see modern wood or brass examples on display in furniture showrooms, and furniture manufacturers are producing modestly sized four-poster beds for the average bedroom. An interesting development has been the production of a 'Four-poster bed Surround Kit' in pine by Richard Burbridge Limited of Oswestry, Shropshire, for use with a modern divan bed.

HOTELS

Many hotels and inns advertise rooms with four-poster or tester beds as an attraction to visitors and the English Tourist Board issues a publication *Hotels and Inns with Four-poster Beds.* This information should also be available from tourist information centres and, in some cases, accommodation lists. Hotels which have these beds include:

Bailiffscourt Hotel, Climping, Littlehampton, West Sussex BN17 5RW. Telephone: 0903 723511.
Baron's Court Hotel, Walsall Wood, Walsall, West Midlands W59 9AH. Telephone: 0543 452020.
The Belfry, Wishaw, Sutton Coldfield, West Midlands B76 9PR. Telephone: 0675 70301.
The Bell Hotel, Market Hill, Clare, Sudbury, Suffolk. Telephone: 0787 277741.
Bibury Court Hotel, Bibury, Cirencester, Gloucestershire, GL7 5NT. Telephone: 028574 337.
Billesley Manor Hotel, Billesley, Alcester, Warwickshire B49 6NF. Telephone: 0789 400888.
Bly House, Chagford, Newton Abbot, Devon. Telephone 06473 2040.
The Charlecote Pheasant, Charlecote, Warwick CV35 9EN. Telephone: 0798 840200.
The Chesterfield Hotel, 11 Great Pulteney Street, Bath, Avon. Telephone: 0225 460953.
The Feathers, Bull Ring, Ludlow, Shropshire SY8 1AA. Telephone: 0584 5261.
Felbridge Hotel, London Road, East Grinstead, West Sussex. Telephone: 0342 26992.

Grasmead House Hotel, 1 Scarcroft Hill, The Mount, York. Telephone: 0904 629996.

Lumley Castle Hotel, Chester-le-Street, County Durham DH3 4NX. Telephone: 091 3891111.

Lygon Arms, Broadway, Worcestershire WR12 7DU. Telephone: 0386 852255.

Manor House Hotel, Moreton-in-Marsh, Gloucestershire GL56 0LJ. Telephone: 0608 50501.

The Mermaid Inn, Mermaid Street, Rye, East Sussex TN31 7EU. Telephone: 0797 223065.

Montagu Arms Hotel, Palace Lane, Beaulieu, Brockenhurst, Hampshire SO42 7ZL. Telephone: 0590 612324.

Mottram Hall Hotel, Mottram St Andrew, Prestbury, Cheshire SK10 4QT. Telephone: 0625 828135.

Riber Hall, Matlock, Derbyshire DE4 5UU. Telephone: 0629 2795.

Royal Crescent Hotel, 16 Royal Crescent, Bath, Avon BA1 2LS. Telephone: 0225 319090.

Seckford Hall Hotel, Woodbridge, Suffolk, IP13 6NU. Telephone: 0394 385678.

Ston Easton Park, Bath, Avon BA3 4DF. Telephone: 076121 631.

The Swan, Bucklow Hill, Knutsford, Cheshire WA16 6RD. Telephone: 0565 830295.

Trebarwith Hotel, Island Estate, Newquay, Cornwall. Telephone: 0637 872288.